CW00509662

Île de Ré

Discovering the Hidden Gems of France's
Idyllic Island Retreat

2024

Travel Guide

Glen B. Smith

Copyright © 2023 by Glen B. Smith

All rights reserved. No part of this publication may be Reproduced, distributed, or transmitted in any form or by Any means, including photocopying, recording, or red Electronic or mechanical methods, without the prior written Permission of the publisher.

Table of content

- Detailed exploration of major villages (Saint-Martin-de-Re, La Flotte, Ars-en-Re)

   - Unique characteristics of each village

   - Local markets and cultural highlights

Chapter 5: Outdoor Activities

   - Cycling routes and bike rentals

   - Beaches (like Le Bois-Plage-en-Re, La Plage de la Cible)

   - Sailing, windsurfing, and other water sports

   - Bird watching and nature reserves

Chapter 6: Culinary Journey

   - Local seafood and specialties

   - Notable restaurants and cafes (e.g., Cote Jardin, George's, La Martiniere)

   - Île de Ré Island Recipes and how to prepare them

  –   Dinning Etiquette

Chapter 7: Cultural Experiences

   - Local arts and crafts

   - Historical museums and exhibitions

   - Seasonal festivals and events

- Local Norms

Chapter 8: Accommodations

- Range from luxury hotels to bed and breakfasts and their cost

- Recommendations for different budgets and preferences

Chapter 9: Practical Information

- Language and currency

- Travel tips and essential information

- Emergency contacts and healthcare facilities

- Do's and Don'ts

Chapter 10: FAQs

- Common questions about travel logistics, activities, and local customs

Map

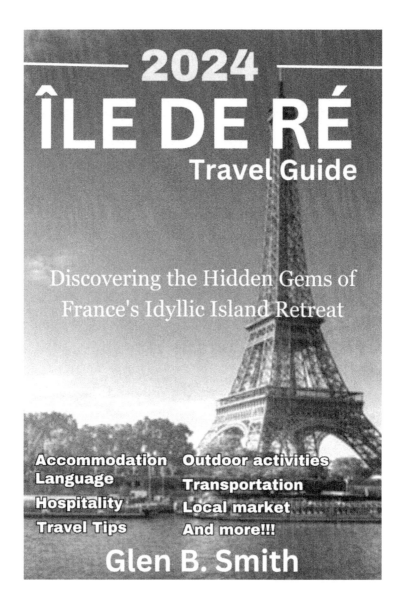

2024

ÎLE DE RÉ
Travel Guide

Discovering the Hidden Gems of
France's Idyllic Island Retreat

Accommodation   Outdoor activities
Language   Transportation
Hospitality   Local market
Travel Tips   And more!!!

Glen B. Smith

Chapter 1: Introduction to Île de Ré

My Memorable Experience at île de Ré Island

I had the privilege of visiting Île de Ré, a picturesque island off the west coast of France, and it was an unforgettable experience that left me with cherished memories.

From the moment I arrived, I was captivated by the island's natural beauty, rich history, and vibrant culture.

One of the most memorable aspects of my trip was the stunning coastline. Île de Ré boasts a coastline adorned with pristine sandy beaches that seem to stretch on endlessly. I spent countless hours basking in the sun, swimming in the crystal-clear waters, and taking leisurely walks along the shore. Each beach had its unique charm, from the bustling beaches near the villages to the secluded coves hidden among the dunes.

Exploring the island by bicycle was another highlight of my visit. Île de Ré is a cyclist's paradise, with a network of well-maintained bike paths that wind through charming villages, vineyards, and salt marshes. I pedaled my way through picturesque lanes lined with hollyhocks, the island's signature flower, and stopped to savor delicious local cuisine in quaint cafés.

The villages on Île de Ré left an indelible mark on my heart. Saint-Martin-de-Ré, with its bustling harbor and historic fortifications, felt like a step back in time. La Flotte, with its colorful fishing boats and lively market, offered a taste of authentic island life. Ars-en-Ré, with its iconic black and white bell tower, exuded charm and serenity.

I couldn't resist indulging in the island's culinary delights. From savory seafood platters filled with oysters, mussels, and shrimp to delectable salt marsh lamb, every meal was a gastronomic delight. The local markets were a treasure trove of fresh produce, artisanal cheeses, and handmade crafts, making for delightful culinary discoveries.

Sunsets on Île de Ré were nothing short of magical. I watched as the sun dipped below the horizon, casting hues of orange and pink across the sky, while the salt marshes glowed in the soft evening light. It was a serene and peaceful moment, a perfect way to end each day.

But it wasn't just the natural beauty and cuisine that made Île de Ré special; it was the warmth and friendliness of the people. Locals welcomed me with open arms, sharing stories of the island's history and traditions. It felt like I was part of a close-knit community, even if only for a short time.

As I reluctantly left Île de Ré, I couldn't help but reflect on the memorable experiences I had on this enchanting island. It was a place where time seemed to slow down, where the simple pleasures of life took center stage, and where I created memories that will stay with me forever. Île de Ré was not just a destination; it was a journey of the heart, and I left with a piece of the island in my soul.

- Overview of the island

Île de Ré, often revered for its unspoiled natural beauty and charming atmosphere, is a picturesque island located off the west coast of France, near La Rochelle. Known for its mild climate and serene landscapes, it's a popular destination for both tourists and locals seeking a peaceful retreat.

Key aspects of Île de Ré include:

1. **Geography and Climate**: The island is characterized by its flat terrain, making it ideal for cycling and walking. Its climate is generally mild, benefiting from the temperate influences of the Atlantic Ocean.

2. **Natural Beauty**: Île de Ré is renowned for its beautiful beaches, salt marshes, and vineyards. The island's coastline

offers a variety of sandy beaches, from popular tourist spots to more secluded areas.

3. **Historical Significance**: The island has a rich history, with landmarks dating back to the Roman era. Notably, the fortifications of Saint-Martin-de-Ré, designed by the famous engineer Vauban, are recognized as a UNESCO World Heritage site.

4. **Cultural Heritage**: The island's villages boast a distinct architectural style, with white-washed houses, colorful shutters, and narrow streets. Local markets, art galleries, and the unique island lifestyle contribute to its cultural richness.

5. **Activities**: Île de Ré is a haven for outdoor enthusiasts, offering activities such as cycling, sailing, and bird watching. Over 100 kilometers of dedicated cycle paths traverse the island, and the shallow waters around the island are ideal for water sports.

6. **Local Cuisine**: The island is also celebrated for its culinary delights, particularly seafood. Fresh oysters and salt harvested from the local marshes are among the delicacies.

7. **Accessibility**: Connected to the mainland by a toll bridge, the island is easily accessible from La Rochelle. Its compact size makes exploration by bike or on foot a preferred mode of travel.

This overview provides a snapshot of Île de Ré's charm and appeal, highlighting why it is a cherished destination for many. For more detailed information and insights into what makes Île de Ré so special, visiting dedicated travel guides and resources is recommended.

– Geographical setting and climate

Île de Ré, a serene and picturesque island, is located off the west coast of France, near La Rochelle in the Atlantic Ocean. Its geographical setting and climate contribute significantly to its appeal as a tourist destination.

Geographical Setting:

- **Location**: The island is situated in the Poitou-Charentes region, nestled in the Bay of Biscay. It is connected to the mainland by a 3 km toll bridge from La Rochelle.

- **Size and Terrain**: Île de Ré is relatively flat, making it ideal for biking and walking. It spans approximately 30 km in length and 5 km in width.

- **Natural Features**: The island is known for its beautiful sandy beaches, salt marshes, and vineyards. Its coastline varies, offering both popular beaches and secluded spots.

Climate:

- General Climate: Île de Ré enjoys a mild oceanic climate, which is influenced by the Atlantic Ocean. The weather is generally temperate throughout the year.

- Seasonal Variations:

 - Summer: The summers are warm and relatively sunny, making it a perfect time for beach activities and outdoor exploration.

 - Winter: Winters are mild and wetter compared to other regions of France. However, the island still retains its charm with quieter and more peaceful landscapes.

 - Spring/Autumn: These seasons are particularly pleasant, with moderate temperatures and fewer tourists, offering a more authentic experience of the island's lifestyle.

This geographical setting and climate make Île de Ré a unique and attractive destination, suitable for a variety of activities and experiences throughout the year. For more detailed information, you can refer to travel guides and meteorological resources specific to the region.

Chapter 2: History

- Roman era to present

The history of Île de Ré spans from the Roman era to the present day, encompassing a rich tapestry of events and transformations:

1. **Roman Era and Early History**: Initially, Île de Ré was known to the Romans as "Rhedon." During this time, it primarily served as a location for salt production, a resource that has historically been crucial to the island's economy.

2. **Middle Ages**: In the medieval period, Île de Ré was a contested site due to its strategic position. This era saw the construction of monasteries and the growth of the salt industry, which continued to be a significant economic driver.

3. **17th Century - Vauban's Fortifications**: A pivotal moment in the island's history came in the 17th century when the famous French military engineer Vauban designed fortifications for Saint-Martin-de-Ré. These fortifications were part of a broader defensive strategy along the French coast and are now listed as a UNESCO World Heritage Site.

4. **19th Century - Economic and Social Developments**: During this time, Île de Ré continued to develop economically with the growth of its salt and wine industries. The construction

of the Phare des Baleines, one of France's tallest lighthouses, marked a significant advancement in the island's maritime history.

5. **20th Century - World Wars and Modernization**: Île de Ré, like much of France, was impacted by the World Wars. The post-war era brought modernization and a gradual shift from traditional industries to tourism, which became a major economic sector.

6. **21st Century - Contemporary Developments**: Today, Île de Ré is known for its natural beauty, historical sites, and as a tranquil holiday destination. Environmental conservation and sustainable tourism are current focuses, ensuring the preservation of the island's unique character and heritage.

This overview presents a brief historical journey of Île de Ré, highlighting key periods and events that have shaped its identity. For a more in-depth understanding of the island's history, consulting specialized historical texts or visiting local museums and historical sites on Île de Ré would provide valuable insights.

- UNESCO World Heritage Sites (like Saint-Martin-de-Ré fortifications)

The fortifications of Saint-Martin-de-Ré on Île de Ré are recognized as a UNESCO World Heritage Site, a designation that underscores their historical and cultural significance:

1. Saint-Martin-de-Ré Fortifications:

- Historical Significance: These fortifications were designed by Sébastien Le Prestre de Vauban, a noted military engineer of King Louis XIV. Vauban's works are celebrated for their innovative approach to fortification and defense.

- **Description**: The fortifications of Saint-Martin-de-Ré consist of ramparts, bastions, and other defensive structures. They were constructed to protect the island from naval assaults, particularly from the British navy during times of conflict.

- **UNESCO Designation:** This site, along with 11 other Vauban sites, was inscribed on the UNESCO World Heritage List in 2008. The designation acknowledges the outstanding universal value of Vauban's fortifications, highlighting their technological innovation and impact on European military architecture.

- **Today's Relevance**: Currently, these fortifications are not only historical landmarks but also tourist attractions that offer insight into the military and architectural history of the period. Their well-preserved state allows visitors to appreciate the complexity and strategic genius of Vauban's designs.

2. Other Notable Sites on Île de Ré:

- While the fortifications of Saint-Martin-de-Ré are the primary UNESCO World Heritage Site on the island, Île de Ré is also home to other historical structures and sites, like the Phare des Baleines lighthouse and the Abbaye des Chateliers, which, while not UNESCO-listed, are integral to the island's rich historical tapestry.

Visiting these sites offers a unique opportunity to delve into the historical narrative of Île de Ré and understand the island's strategic importance through various eras. For more information and details on visiting these sites, consulting travel guides or the official UNESCO website would be beneficial.

- Notable historical structures (e.g., Phare des Baleines lighthouse, Abbaye des Chateliers)

Île de Ré is home to several notable historical structures that reflect its rich heritage:

1. **Phare des Baleines Lighthouse**:

   - **Location and History**: Situated at the westernmost tip of the island, the Phare des Baleines was constructed in 1854 to replace an earlier lighthouse from the 17th century. Its name, meaning "Whales Lighthouse," originates from the frequent sighting of whales in the area during earlier times.

- **Features**: The lighthouse stands at an impressive height, offering panoramic views of the island and the surrounding sea. Visitors can climb the 257 steps to the top for a spectacular vantage point.

- **Significance**: Beyond its navigational purpose, the lighthouse serves as a historical monument, reflecting the maritime heritage of Île de Ré. It also includes a museum detailing the history of the lighthouse and its role in maritime navigation.

2. Abbaye des Chateliers:

- **Background**: The Abbaye des Chateliers, located near La Flotte, is a ruined Cistercian abbey dating back to the 12th century.

- **Architecture**: Although in ruins, the abbey's remnants showcase the early Gothic architectural style. It was once a significant religious and economic center, involved in salt and wine production.

- **Current State**: Today, the site is open to the public and stands as a testament to the medieval ecclesiastical history of the island. Its picturesque setting amidst the natural landscape makes it a popular spot for visitors and photographers.

These historical structures not only add to the charm of Île de Ré but also provide insights into its past, from medieval times to the 19th century. They are integral parts of the island's cultural landscape and are worth exploring for anyone interested in history and architecture. For more detailed information and visiting guidelines, it's advisable to consult local travel resources or historical guides specific to Île de Ré.

Chapter 3: Getting There and Around

– Access via La Rochelle

Accessing Île de Ré from La Rochelle is straightforward, with various transport options available to suit different needs and budgets. Here's a detailed overview:

By Bridge:

The Île de Ré is connected to La Rochelle by a 3 km bridge that is accessible 24/7. This bridge allows for the passage of cars, campervans, and motorbikes, with specific toll charges based on the season:

- Cars: €8 during off-peak season (September 12 to June 19) and €16 during peak season (June 20 to September 11).
- Motorcycles: A fee of €3 is applicable for motorcycles crossing the bridge.
- Pedestrians and Bicyclists: Cross for free at any time, encouraging eco-friendly travel.

Public Transport Options and Costs:

Île de Ré is well-served by public transport from La Rochelle, offering economical and convenient options for visitors:

- Bus Line 3/3E: This line runs from La Rochelle train station to various destinations across the island. Single journey tickets cost €2.30, while return tickets are priced at €4.10. For frequent travelers, there are weekly and monthly passes available, which provide unlimited travel and can offer significant savings.

- RespiRé Shuttle: In the high season, a shuttle service operates between La Rochelle and Île de Ré at a cost of €1 per trip. This shuttle is particularly useful for cyclists as it can transport bicycles.

These travel options provide a range of prices and conveniences, catering to different preferences and ensuring that travelers can reach Île de Ré from La Rochelle with ease. Whether opting for the autonomy of driving across the bridge or the affordability and convenience of public transport, there are choices to fit every visitor's needs.

- Airport

La Rochelle - Île de Ré Airport, officially known as Aéroport de La Rochelle - Île de Ré (IATA: LRH), is a key gateway for travelers heading to Île de Ré. The airport is conveniently located near La Rochelle, just a short drive from the bridge that connects to Île de Ré. Here is a detailed overview of the airport and its facilities:

Location and Access

The airport is situated approximately 5 kilometers from La Rochelle city center and about 13 kilometers from Île de Ré, making it easily accessible by road. The journey from the airport to Île de Ré can typically be completed within 20 minutes by car or taxi.

Facilities and Services

- Terminals: The airport has a single terminal that handles both domestic and international flights.

- Airlines: It serves as a base for various airlines including easyJet, Ryanair, and others, offering flights to cities across Europe such as London, Brussels, and Dublin .

- Passenger Services: Facilities at the airport include car rental agencies, a few shops and dining options, luggage services, and free WiFi. There is also ample parking available for those who are driving.

Transportation to Île de Ré

- By Car: Renting a car or taking a taxi are the most direct options for reaching Île de Ré from the airport. The drive takes about 20 minutes, and taxi fares typically range around €50, depending on the exact destination on the island .

- Public Transport: There is no direct bus service from the airport to Île de Ré, but travelers can take a bus to La Rochelle city center and then connect to Île de Ré via another bus or shuttle. The total journey time will vary depending on connections.

Operational Details

- Runway: The airport has one runway that accommodates all types of aircraft used by the airlines operating here.

- Navigation Aids: It is equipped with modern navigational aids to ensure the safety of flights arriving and departing under various weather conditions .

Aéroport de La Rochelle - Île de Ré

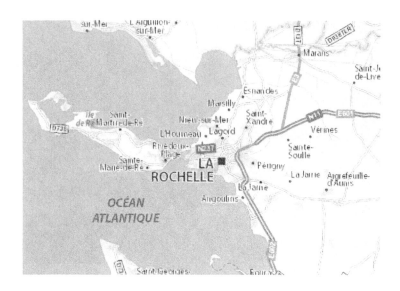

La Rochelle - Île de Ré Airport is a convenient entry point for visitors to the region, offering a range of services to facilitate easy access to Île de Ré and the surrounding areas. Its proximity to major European cities also makes it an ideal starting point for exploring the scenic beauty of France's Atlantic coast.

- Transportation options (e.g., cycling, car travel)

Île de Ré, a popular French island located off the west coast of France, offers a variety of transportation options suitable for all types of travelers. Here's a comprehensive overview of the main transport methods available on the island, along with associated costs:

Cycling

Cycling is one of the most popular ways to explore Île de Ré, thanks to over 100 kilometers of flat, well-maintained cycle paths that cover the island. These paths provide a scenic and eco-friendly way to visit different villages and beaches.

- Rental Costs: Bike rental shops are abundant, and you can rent a bike for around €12 to €20 per day. Discounts may be available for longer rentals.

Car Travel

Driving is another viable option, particularly for families carrying beach gear or those who prefer not to cycle. The island is accessible via a toll bridge from La Rochelle.

- Bridge Toll: The cost of the toll bridge varies seasonally; it's around €16 during the summer months and €8 in the off-season for cars. This fee includes return trips.

- Car Rental: Available at La Rochelle Airport and in various locations in La Rochelle, car rental prices vary widely depending on the season and the type of vehicle, but generally start from about €30 per day.

Electric Vehicles

Île de Ré encourages the use of electric vehicles (EVs) with several charging stations around the island. Renting an electric bike or scooter can be a fun and sustainable way to get around.
- Rental Costs: Renting an electric bike can cost approximately €25 to €35 per day.

Public Transport

The local bus service, called Les Mouettes, connects La Rochelle to Île de Ré and also circulates around the island, linking various villages.
- Bus Fare: A single bus ticket costs around €1.30, making it an economical option for getting around. There are also travel passes available that offer unlimited travel for a set number of days.

Taxis and Shuttles

Taxis are available for direct, private transport from La Rochelle Airport to Île de Ré, or for traveling within the island.
- Taxi Costs: A typical taxi ride from La Rochelle Airport to Île de Ré can cost about €50. On the island, taxi fares depend on the distance but expect to pay a premium for the convenience.

These transportation options provide flexibility and convenience for visitors to Île de Ré, allowing them to choose the best mode of travel to suit their preferences and budget.

Whether opting for the independence of car travel or the leisurely pace of cycling, Île de Ré's transport infrastructure supports a smooth and enjoyable visit.

– Details on the toll bridge (Pont de l'île de Ré)

The Pont de l'île de Ré is a critical structure connecting Île de Ré to the mainland at La Rochelle. Here are some key details about this toll bridge:

1. **Construction and Length**:

   - The bridge was completed in 1988, offering a direct link to the island from La Rochelle.

   - It spans approximately 3 km, making it a significant engineering feat.

2. **Toll Charges:**

   - There is a toll for vehicles to cross the bridge, with the fee varying depending on the type of vehicle and the season. Generally, the toll is higher during the peak tourist season (from April to September).

   - Payment methods include card and cash, and the toll is collected while entering the island.

3. **Impact on Accessibility**:

27

- The construction of the bridge significantly improved access to Île de Ré, making it more convenient for visitors and residents to travel between the island and the mainland.

- It replaced the earlier ferry service, providing a more reliable and quicker means of transportation.

4. **Strategic Importance**:

- The bridge not only facilitates tourism but also supports the local economy by enabling easier transport of goods and services.

5. **Traffic Considerations**:

- During the summer months and holiday periods, the bridge can experience heavy traffic. It's advisable to plan travel times to avoid peak hours.

6. **Scenic Route**:

- Crossing the bridge offers scenic views of the ocean and is often the first memorable experience for visitors arriving on the island.

For the most current information on toll charges and traffic conditions, it's recommended to check official sources or local travel guides before planning your trip to Île de Ré.

– Entry requirements

Traveling to Île de Ré, which is part of France, involves adhering to the general entry requirements set by the French government for international visitors. Here's a detailed and comprehensive guide on what documents are required:

Passport and Visa Requirements

1. Passports: All travelers entering France, including those visiting Île de Ré, must have a valid passport. The passport should be valid for at least three months beyond the period of intended stay. It's advised to have a passport with at least six months of validity to avoid any issues at the border.

2. Visas: Whether you need a visa depends on your nationality and the length of your stay:

  - EU/EEA/Swiss Citizens: No visa required.

  - Non-EU Citizens: Most non-EU citizens who wish to stay in France for short visits (up to 90 days within a 180-day period) do not need a visa if they are from visa-exempt countries such as the USA, Canada, Australia, and Japan. For longer stays, a visa is required.

  - Visa Requirements for Other Nationals: Citizens from countries not under the visa exemption agreement with the Schengen Area will need to apply for a Schengen visa for short stays. This can be done through the French consulate or embassy in their home country.

Customs Regulations

Upon entering France, travelers may need to declare certain items at customs, especially if carrying items above a certain value (generally 430€ for air and sea travelers, and 300€ for others). Prohibited items include but are not limited to drugs, weapons, and certain food products. It's advisable to check the detailed list on the French Customs official website for specific items and their allowances.

Health and Insurance Requirements

- Health Insurance: All visitors to France should have travel health insurance covering all medical expenses, including emergency repatriation, due to any reason (e.g., accident, illness). This is particularly important for non-EU travelers who are not covered under any European health schemes.

Additional Tips

- Identification: Always carry a form of identification with you, as local authorities may ask to see it at any time.
- Driving Licenses: If you plan to rent a car and drive in France, a valid driver's license from your country is usually acceptable, but it's often recommended to obtain an international driving permit.

- Children's Travel: Children should have their own passport. If traveling with one parent or someone who is not their parent, a signed letter of authorization from the other parent or legal guardians may be required.

Before traveling, always check the most current information with the French consulate or embassy or visit the French visa official website for detailed and updated requirements. This will help ensure that you have all the necessary documents and meet all legal requirements for your trip to Île de Ré.

– Recommendations for stops along the way (like Rouen)

When traveling to Île de Ré, especially if you're coming from the UK or other parts of Europe, there are several noteworthy stops you might consider along the way to enrich your journey:

1. **Rouen**:

   - **Historical Significance**: Known for its rich history, Rouen is a charming city along the River Seine in Normandy. It's famous for its stunning Gothic architecture, including the Notre-Dame Cathedral.

- **Cultural Attractions**: Explore the historic old town, the place where Joan of Arc was martyred, and numerous museums and art galleries.

2. **Nantes:**

- **Cultural Hub**: This vibrant city is known for its rich history and contemporary art scene. Don't miss the unique mechanical elephant at Les Machines de l'île.

- **Gastronomy**: Nantes offers a variety of culinary delights, particularly seafood and local wines.

3. **La Rochelle:**

- **Gateway to Île de Ré:** Before crossing the bridge to the island, La Rochelle itself is worth exploring. Known for its picturesque old harbor and historic towers.

- **Aquarium**: One of Europe's largest private aquariums, offering an extensive collection of marine life.

4. **Cognac:**

- **Famous for Brandy**: If you have a penchant for spirits, a detour to the town of Cognac to visit one of its renowned distilleries could be a highlight.

- **Historic Town**: The old town is a delightful area to stroll through, with its traditional architecture and quaint streets.

5. **Saintes:**

- **Ancient History:** This town is known for its Romanesque architecture and ancient ruins, including an amphitheater.

- **Scenic Views**: Enjoy a walk along the Charente River for some beautiful views.

6. **Poitiers:**

- **Medieval Architecture**: Poitiers is famous for its preserved medieval architecture and historic churches.

- **Futuroscope**: A theme park focused on futuristic multimedia, cinematographic and audio-visual techniques.

7. **Bordeaux:**

- **Wine Capital:** Renowned for its wine, Bordeaux is a must-visit for wine enthusiasts.

- **UNESCO World Heritage Site**: The city center is a UNESCO site, known for its neoclassical architecture.

Each of these destinations offers unique experiences and can add significant value to your trip to Île de Ré. Depending on your route and interests, you can tailor your itinerary to include these culturally rich and scenic stops.

Chapter 4: Villages of Île de Ré

- Detailed exploration of major villages (Saint-Martin-de-Re, La Flotte, Ars-en-Re)

Exploring the major villages of Île de Ré, such as Saint-Martin-de-Re, La Flotte, and Ars-en-Re, reveals the unique charm and cultural richness of the island:

1. Saint-Martin-de-Re:

- **Capital and Historical Center**: As the capital of Île de Ré, Saint-Martin-de-Re is known for its historical significance, including the Vauban fortifications, which are a UNESCO World Heritage site.

- **Vibrant Harbor and Shops**: The village boasts a lively harbor surrounded by quaint shops and eateries. Its streets are lined with beautiful old buildings, making it a picturesque spot for leisurely strolls.

- **Cultural Attractions**: Visitors can explore landmarks like the Ernest Cognacq Museum and enjoy the local market for regional specialties.

2. **La Flotte:**

- **Medieval Charm:** This village is recognized for its medieval history and architecture, with a beautiful harbor that's a hub for cafes and ice cream parlors.

- **Market and Local Crafts**: La Flotte hosts a popular street market where you can find local produce and artisan crafts.

- **Beach and Leisure Activities**: The beach at La Flotte offers a relaxing spot for visitors, and there are also opportunities for sailing and other water sports.

3. **Ars-en-Re:**

- **Distinctive Architecture**: Known for its iconic church steeple, which served as a landmark for sailors, Ars-en-Re is characterized by its traditional white houses with colorful shutters.

- **Art and Antiques**: The village is a haven for art lovers, with several galleries and antique shops.

- **Natural Beauty**: The surrounding salt marshes and beaches offer a tranquil setting for nature walks and birdwatching.

Each village on Île de Ré has its own unique character and charm, offering visitors a diverse range of experiences from historical exploration to relaxing by the sea. For a more immersive experience, spending time in these villages allows you to soak in the local culture, cuisine, and stunning landscapes that make Île de Ré a special destination.

– Unique characteristics of each village

Each village on Île de Ré has its own unique characteristics and charm:

1. **Saint-Martin-de-Re:**

 - **Historical Significance**: Known for its UNESCO-listed Vauban fortifications, this village has a rich history evident in its architecture and layout.

 - **Vibrant Harbor**: The harbor area is bustling with activity, surrounded by numerous shops, cafes, and restaurants, making it a lively center for visitors and locals.

 - **Cultural Hub**: With museums like the Ernest Cognacq Museum and frequent cultural events, Saint-Martin-de-Re offers a deep dive into the island's history and culture.

2. **La Flotte:**

 - **Medieval Ambiance**: La Flotte is recognized for its medieval market and beautiful harbor, offering a glimpse into the past with its charming streets and traditional architecture.

- **Artisanal Shops and Market**: This village is famous for its daily market where you can explore a variety of local products, from fresh produce to artisan crafts.

- **Scenic Waterfront**: The waterfront area is ideal for leisurely walks, offering picturesque views and a relaxed atmosphere.

3. **Ars-en-Re:**

- **Iconic Church Steeple**: Its church steeple, painted in black and white, is a distinctive landmark and was historically used as a guide for sailors.

- **Artistic Flair**: Ars-en-Re is known for its art galleries and antique shops, making it a great destination for art enthusiasts.

- **Natural Beauty**: The surrounding salt marshes and beaches provide a tranquil setting for nature walks and bird watching, highlighting the village's connection to its natural environment.

These villages, with their distinct features, contribute to the rich tapestry of Île de Ré, offering visitors diverse experiences from historical explorations to enjoying local culinary delights and artisan crafts.

– Local markets and cultural highlights

The local markets and cultural highlights of Île de Ré are integral to its charm and appeal, offering visitors a taste of local life and tradition:

1. **Local Markets:**

- **Saint-Martin-de-Re**: This market is known for its vibrant atmosphere and variety of stalls selling everything from fresh local produce to crafts and clothing. It's a great place to sample regional specialties.

- **La Flotte:** Home to a medieval market, La Flotte offers a unique shopping experience with its array of local food products, artisanal goods, and souvenirs.

- **Ars-en-Re:** This market is smaller but notable for its authentic local feel, offering fresh produce, seafood, and regional delicacies.

2. **Cultural Highlights:**

- **Festivals and Events**: Île de Ré hosts various cultural events and festivals throughout the year, celebrating everything from music to local food and traditional crafts.

- **Museums and Galleries**: The Ernest Cognacq Museum in Saint-Martin-de-Re provides insights into the island's history and culture. Art galleries across the island showcase local and regional artists.

- **Historical Sites**: The fortifications in Saint-Martin-de-Re, the Phare des Baleines lighthouse, and the Abbaye des Chateliers are notable historical sites that offer a glimpse into the island's past.

- **Culinary Experiences**: Seafood is a staple of the local cuisine, with oysters and salt from the island's marshes being particularly famous. Many restaurants and cafes offer traditional French and regional dishes.

These markets and cultural offerings not only provide entertainment and shopping opportunities but also help preserve and celebrate the rich heritage and traditions of Île de Ré. For visitors, they offer an immersive experience into the local way of life, making a trip to Île de Ré both enjoyable and culturally enriching.

Chapter 5: Outdoor Activities

- Cycling routes and bike rentals

Cycling is a popular and enjoyable way to explore Île de Ré, thanks to its flat terrain and extensive network of bike paths:

1. **Cycling Routes:**

- **Island-Wide Network**: Île de Ré features over 100 kilometers of cycle paths, connecting various villages and attractions across the island.

- **Scenic Trails**: The routes offer scenic views, passing through vineyards, beaches, forests, and salt marshes. Popular trails include the route from Saint-Martin-de-Re to the Phare des Baleines lighthouse and the paths leading to the beaches.

- **Family-Friendly**: Due to the flat landscape and well-maintained paths, the routes are suitable for all ages and abilities, making them ideal for family outings.

2. **Bike Rentals:**

- **Availability**: Numerous bike rental shops are scattered throughout the island, with outlets in most major villages like Saint-Martin-de-Re, La Flotte, and Ars-en-Re.

- **Variety of Bikes**: These shops offer a wide range of bicycles, including standard bikes, electric bikes, children's bikes, and bikes with trailers for young children.

- **Services**: Many rental services also offer helmets, locks, and maps, and some provide repair services in case of any issues during your cycling adventures.

3. **Tips for Cyclists:**

- **Reservations**: During peak tourist seasons, it's advisable to book your bikes in advance.

- **Safety**: Always follow local cycling regulations, wear a helmet, and be mindful of pedestrians and vehicle traffic where paths intersect roads.

- **Navigation**: Carry a map or use a GPS device, as some routes may traverse through less populated areas of the island.

Cycling on Île de Ré not only offers a healthy and eco-friendly way to travel but also allows you to experience the island's natural beauty and charm at your own pace.

- Beaches (like Le Bois-Plage-en-Re, La Plage de la Cible)

Île de Ré boasts a variety of beautiful beaches, each offering its own unique experience:

1. Le Bois-Plage-en-Re:

- **Popular and Lively**: This beach is one of the most popular on the island, known for its wide stretches of sand and lively atmosphere.

- **Family-Friendly**: It's a great choice for families, offering plenty of space for beach activities and swimming.

- Amenities: The beach is well-equipped with facilities such as showers, toilets, and nearby restaurants.

2. La Plage de la Cible:

- **Proximity to Saint-Martin-de-Re**: Close to the capital, this beach is easily accessible and ideal for those staying in or near Saint-Martin-de-Re.

- **Facilities**: It offers good amenities, including a beach restaurant/bar and lifeguard services during the summer.

- **Watersports:** The conditions here are favorable for various watersports, making it a hit among more active beachgoers.

3. **Other Notable Beaches:**

- **Plage des Grenettes**: Known for its surfing opportunities, this beach is a bit more secluded and offers a more natural setting.

- **Plage de Trousse Chemise**: Located near Les Portes-en-Re, this beach is appreciated for its tranquility and natural beauty, ideal for a peaceful day by the sea.

- **Plage de Gros Jonc**: This is another family-friendly beach, suitable for both sunbathing and surfing.

Each of these beaches has its own character and charm, catering to different preferences, whether you're looking for vibrant beach life, watersports, or a quiet spot to relax. Remember to respect the natural environment and local regulations when visiting the beaches.

- Sailing, windsurfing, and other water sports

Île de Ré is a haven for water sports enthusiasts, offering a range of activities to enjoy the island's beautiful coastal settings:

1. **Sailing**:

- The island's harbors, particularly in Saint-Martin-de-Re and La Flotte, are ideal for sailing.

- Sailing schools and clubs offer courses and rentals for both beginners and experienced sailors.

- The calm waters around Île de Ré make it perfect for leisurely sailing excursions.

2. **Windsurfing**:

- Windsurfing is a popular activity on the island, with suitable wind conditions for both beginners and advanced windsurfers.

- There are several spots around the island, such as the beaches at Le Bois-Plage-en-Re and La Couarde-sur-Mer, known for their excellent windsurfing conditions.

- Equipment rental and lessons are available at various locations on the island.

3. **Other Water Sports:**

- **Kitesurfing**: This is another thrilling sport enjoyed on the island, with Plage de Gros Jonc being a notable spot for kitesurfing enthusiasts.

- Stand Up Paddleboarding (SUP): For a more relaxed experience, SUP is a great way to explore the coastlines and beaches of Île de Ré.

- **Kayaking**: Exploring the island's beaches and marshes by kayak offers a unique perspective of its natural beauty.

These activities not only provide an adrenaline rush but also allow visitors to connect with the natural maritime environment of Île de Ré. Many local businesses cater to water sports enthusiasts, offering equipment hire and lessons to ensure a safe and enjoyable experience.

– Bird watching and nature reserves

Île de Ré is an excellent destination for bird watching and exploring nature reserves, offering rich biodiversity and unique ecosystems:

1. **Lilleau des Niges Nature Reserve:**

   - Located in the northern part of the island near Ars-en-Ré, this reserve is a key site for bird watching.

- It's particularly famous for its salt marshes, which attract a wide variety of migratory birds.

- The reserve is managed by the Ligue pour la Protection des Oiseaux (LPO), and visitors can enjoy guided tours to learn about the local birdlife and habitats.

2. **Bird Watching Opportunities:**

- Île de Ré's diverse landscapes, including beaches, forests, and marshes, provide ideal habitats for numerous bird species.

- Species commonly seen include waders, seabirds, and songbirds. The island is a stopover point for many migratory birds, making it a dynamic place for bird watching throughout the year.

- Some popular bird watching spots are along the beaches and coastal paths, where you can observe seabirds and shorebirds.

3. **Nature Trails and Walks:**

- The island offers several nature trails that wind through different habitats, providing opportunities to explore and observe local flora and fauna.

- These trails are suitable for all ages and offer a peaceful way to connect with the island's natural environment.

4. **Conservation Efforts**:

- The island is involved in various conservation efforts to protect its natural landscapes and wildlife, emphasizing sustainable tourism practices.

For nature lovers and bird watchers, Île de Ré presents an unspoiled natural environment to enjoy. The island's commitment to conservation ensures that its natural beauty and wildlife can be appreciated by visitors for years to come.

Chapter 6: Culinary Journey

- Local seafood and specialties

Île de Ré is renowned for its exquisite local seafood and specialties that reflect its rich maritime culture and traditional culinary practices:

1. **Oysters**: Oysters are a specialty of Île de Ré and have been a significant part of the island's maritime culture for centuries. The flavor of Île de Ré oysters varies depending on their farming conditions, such as being farmed on rocks or sand, and they are enjoyed year-round. You can find various oyster huts around the island offering fresh oysters along with other seafood delights.

2. **Salt and Salted Products**: The island is also known for its salt production, particularly the Fleur de Sel. This hand-harvested sea salt is a gourmet product, treasured for its delicate flavor and texture. Artisanal products like salted butter caramel made with this local salt are popular among visitors.

3. **Local Sweets and Desserts:** Île de Ré offers unique sweet treats like jams made with seasonal fruits and special creations such as 'Rétaise' jam, a combination of melon, green tomato,

orange, and lemon. Local artisanal ice creams, including unique flavors like oyster, are a must-try.

4. **Chocolates with a Local Twist**: Artisan chocolatiers on the island create special chocolates using local ingredients, such as Charentes-Poitou PDO butter and Île de Ré sea salt. These chocolates often incorporate interesting combinations, like sea salt flavored ganache.

5. **Exceptional Cheeses**: Île de Ré has its own goat cheese varieties, offering a superb range of traditional and gourmet cheeses. Tasting these fresh cheeses, including ones flavored with local ingredients like Espelette pepper or fennel, is a real treat.

6. **Honey and Honey Products**: The island's beekeepers produce local Île de Ré honey and other honey-based products. These include homemade gingerbread, royal jelly, and even honey vinegar with samphire.

7. **Local Wines and Beverages**: The island's wine merchant offers a selection of local wines, pineaux, and cognacs, as well as high-quality wines from other regions of France. Local craft breweries on the island produce beers using traditional methods, with flavors capturing the essence of the sea.

These culinary highlights make Île de Ré a paradise for food enthusiasts, offering a taste of the island's rich gastronomic heritage and natural bounty.

– Notable restaurants and cafes (e.g., Cote Jardin, George's, La Martiniere)

Île de Ré offers a delightful array of restaurants and cafes, each bringing its own unique flavor and ambiance. Here are some notable options for dining:

1. **Julie Dans la Cuisine**: This cozy family restaurant, located away from the city center, specializes in traditional French cuisine with a focus on fresh, local products. It's highly recommended for its range of artistically prepared dishes, including seafood and veal entrecote on charcoal.

2. **L'Ecailler**: Situated in the city center in one of the most historic buildings in the port, L'Ecailler is known for its elegant atmosphere and delicious seafood dishes. The menu includes tuna steaks, oysters, yellowfin tuna, wild turbot, roasted mullet, monkfish, and more.

3. **Le Balaou**: A family-oriented restaurant a short walk from the beach, Le Balaou is praised for dishes like Accras de morue

(codfish accras) and lemon mojito tart. It's also known for its friendly service.

4. **La Table d'Olivia**: Often claimed to be the best restaurant in Saint-Martin-de Ré, La Table d'Olivia specializes in refined seafood dishes and authentic cuisine that honors local products. The restaurant is also noted for its elegant-vintage interior and beautiful garden.

5. **La Cabane du Feneau**: Offering a rustic beach restaurant vibe, La Cabane du Feneau is run by the Palvadeau brothers and serves fresh and gourmet dishes with a "guinguette" character, in the heart of the island's marshes.

6. **La Rhetaise**: Located in a beautiful salt marshland landscape, La Rhetaise is perfect for enjoying the best oysters, clams, mussels, and imperial shrimps on the island.

7. **Christopher Coutanceau**: A three-star Michelin restaurant in La Rochelle, offering unique and authentic dishes, Christopher Coutanceau is known for its exceptional products, pure flavors, and outstanding presentations.

8. **Ben-Hur Char 'a Huitres**: A quaint seafood restaurant, Ben-Hur Char 'a Huitres invites guests to feast on delicious fresh products and seafood tapas, all "home-made", in a cozy setting with a lovely terrace.

9. **Restaurant bistronomique la Salicorne**: An urban-style restaurant in the heart of the city, La Salicorne offers a modern-

loft design and dishes that are regularly redesigned, featuring a variety of creative options.

Each of these restaurants provides a unique dining experience, reflecting the rich culinary heritage of Île de Ré. Whether you're looking for traditional French cuisine, fresh seafood, or a cozy atmosphere, these establishments are sure to delight your palate.

- Île de Ré Island Recipes and how to prepare them

Île de Ré, located off the west coast of France, is renowned for its delicious cuisine, featuring fresh seafood, locally grown vegetables, and flavorful herbs. Here are three traditional recipes from Île de Ré along with their ingredients and preparation methods:

1. Mouclade de l'île de Ré (Mussels with Curry Sauce)

Ingredients:

- 2 kg fresh mussels
- 2 onions, finely chopped
- 2 cloves of garlic, minced
- 1 tbsp olive oil
- 1 tbsp curry powder
- 200 ml dry white wine
- 200 ml heavy cream
- Salt and pepper to taste
- Chopped parsley for garnish

Preparation:

1. Clean the mussels under cold water, scrubbing the shells and removing the beards.

2. In a large pot, sauté the onions and garlic in olive oil until translucent.

3. Add the curry powder and cook for another minute.

4. Pour in the white wine and bring to a boil.

5. Add the mussels, cover, and steam for about 5 minutes, or until the mussels open.

6. Remove the mussels from the pot and set aside.

7. Add the cream to the pot and simmer until the sauce thickens slightly.

8. Season with salt and pepper to taste.

9. Pour the sauce over the mussels and garnish with chopped parsley.

2. Tarte aux Pommes de l'île de Ré (Île de Ré Apple Tart)

Ingredients:

- 1 sheet of puff pastry

- 4-5 apples, peeled, cored, and thinly sliced

- 100 g sugar

- 1 tsp cinnamon

- 1 egg, beaten (for egg wash)

Preparation:

1. Preheat the oven to 180°C (350°F).

2. Roll out the puff pastry and place it in a tart pan.

3. Arrange the apple slices in a circular pattern on top of the pastry.

4. Sprinkle sugar and cinnamon over the apples.

5. Brush the edges of the pastry with the beaten egg.

6. Bake for 30-40 minutes, or until the pastry is golden and the apples are tender.

7. Serve warm with a dollop of whipped cream or vanilla ice cream.

3. Pommes de Terre à la Bonnotte (Bonnotte Potatoes)

Ingredients:

- 1 kg Bonnotte potatoes (or any small, waxy potato)

- 50 g butter

- Salt and pepper to taste

- Chopped chives for garnish

Preparation:

1. Wash the potatoes and place them in a large pot.

2. Cover with cold water and add a pinch of salt.

3. Bring to a boil and cook until the potatoes are tender.

4. Drain the potatoes and let them cool slightly.

5. In a large skillet, melt the butter over medium heat.

6. Add the potatoes to the skillet and cook until golden brown, turning occasionally.

7. Season with salt and pepper.

8. Garnish with chopped chives before serving.

4. Caramelized Onion and Goat Cheese Tart

Ingredients:

- 1 sheet of puff pastry

- 3 large onions, thinly sliced

- 100 g goat cheese, crumbled

- 2 tbsp olive oil

- 1 tbsp brown sugar

- Salt and pepper to taste

- Fresh thyme leaves for garnish

Preparation:

1. Preheat the oven to 180°C (350°F).

61

2. In a large skillet, heat olive oil over medium heat.

3. Add the sliced onions and cook, stirring occasionally, until caramelized (about 20-30 minutes).

4. Stir in the brown sugar and season with salt and pepper.

5. Roll out the puff pastry and place it in a tart pan.

6. Spread the caramelized onions evenly over the pastry.

7. Sprinkle the crumbled goat cheese on top.

8. Bake for 25-30 minutes, or until the pastry is golden and the cheese is melted.

9. Garnish with fresh thyme leaves before serving.

5. Pêches de Vigne Flambées au Cognac (Flambéed Vineyard Peaches)

Ingredients:

- 4 ripe vineyard peaches, halved and pitted
- 50 g butter
- 2 tbsp brown sugar
- 60 ml cognac
- Vanilla ice cream for serving

Preparation:

1. In a large skillet, melt the butter over medium heat.

2. Add the peach halves, cut side down, and cook until caramelized (about 5 minutes).

3. Sprinkle the brown sugar over the peaches and cook for another minute.

4. Carefully pour the cognac over the peaches and ignite with a long match.

5. Allow the flames to die down naturally.

6. Serve the flambéed peaches warm with a scoop of vanilla ice cream.

These recipes showcase the delicious flavors of Île de Ré and are perfect for enjoying a taste of the island's culinary delights at home.

– Île de Ré Island Dining Etiquette

Dining etiquette on Île de Ré Island, France, reflects the country's rich culinary tradition and emphasis on enjoying good food in good company. Here are some key points to keep in mind when dining on the island:

Before the Meal:

1. Reservations: It's advisable to make reservations, especially during peak tourist seasons or for popular restaurants, to ensure a table.

2. Arrival Time: Arriving on time for your reservation shows respect for the restaurant staff and other diners.

3. Dress Code: While the dress code is generally casual on the island, it's respectful to dress neatly when dining out.

Seating and Ordering:

1. Seating: Wait to be seated by the host or hostess, especially in more formal establishments.

2. Menu: Take your time to peruse the menu and ask the server for recommendations if needed.

3. Ordering: When ready, signal the server by making eye contact or raising your hand to indicate that you're ready to order.

During the Meal:

1. Bread Etiquette: Bread is typically served with meals. Tear off a small piece of bread and place it on the edge of your plate, rather than directly on the table.

2. Eating Pace: French dining is often leisurely, so take your time to savor each course and enjoy the experience.

3. Wine Pairing: Wine is an integral part of French dining. If unsure, ask the server for wine recommendations to complement your meal.

4. Cutlery Usage: Start with the outermost utensils and work your way in with each course. Keep your hands visible above the table at all times.

5. Table Manners: Keep your elbows off the table and refrain from slurping or making loud noises while eating.

6. Tipping: While a service charge is often included in the bill, it's customary to leave a small additional tip for good service (around 5-10%).

After the Meal:

1. Payment: Wait for the server to bring the bill to your table. You can pay by cash or card, and it's customary to pay for your entire group together.

2. Saying Thank You: A simple "merci" (thank you) to the server is appreciated as you leave the restaurant.

Cultural Considerations:

1. Language: While English is spoken in many tourist areas, attempting to speak French, even just a few words, is appreciated.

2. Respect for Food: Finish the food on your plate as wasting food is considered disrespectful in French culture.

3. Dining Hours: Note that dining times may differ from other countries, with lunch typically served between 12:00 p.m. and 2:00 p.m., and dinner between 7:00 p.m. and 9:00 p.m.

By following these dining etiquette guidelines, you can enjoy a pleasant and respectful dining experience on Île de Ré Island, France, and appreciate the island's culinary offerings to the fullest.

Chapter 7: Cultural Experiences

- Local arts and crafts

Île de Ré is not only known for its natural beauty and cuisine but also for its vibrant arts and crafts scene. Here are some local arts and crafts you can explore on the island:

1. **Pottery and Ceramics**: Île de Ré has several pottery workshops where you can discover beautifully crafted ceramics. You can find decorative pieces, tableware, and unique souvenirs with intricate designs inspired by the island's surroundings.

2. **Painting and Art Galleries**: The island's picturesque landscapes and charming villages have inspired many artists. You can explore local art galleries showcasing paintings, sculptures, and other forms of visual art created by both resident and visiting artists.

3. **Handmade Jewelry**: Look for artisan jewelry shops offering handcrafted pieces made from various materials, including seashells, glass beads, and semi-precious stones. These unique creations capture the essence of the island.

4. **Textile and Fabric Crafts**: Île de Ré has a tradition of textile crafts, including weaving and embroidery. Visit boutique shops to find locally made clothing, accessories, and home textiles with a coastal and maritime theme.

5. **Woodworking**: Some craftsmen on the island specialize in woodworking. You can find hand-carved wooden items, including furniture, decorative objects, and even model boats.

6. **Fishing Nets and Nautical Decor**: Given its maritime heritage, the island offers an abundance of nautical-themed crafts. Look for shops selling fishing nets, ropes, and maritime decorations that make for unique souvenirs.

7. **Glassblowing**: Some artisans practice the art of glassblowing, creating delicate glassware and decorative pieces. You may even have the opportunity to watch glassblowers at work in their studios.

8. **Local Markets**: Local markets, especially in Saint-Martin-de-Ré and La Flotte, often feature stalls selling handmade crafts. These markets are excellent places to discover unique creations from local artists and artisans.

9. **Workshops and Classes**: If you're interested in learning some of these crafts yourself, consider taking a workshop or class. Many artists and artisans offer hands-on experiences where you can create your own piece of art or craft.

Exploring the arts and crafts scene on Île de Ré allows you to appreciate the creativity and talent of the island's residents while bringing home a piece of the island's unique culture.

– Historical museums and exhibitions

Île de Ré offers a fascinating journey through its history and culture via its historical museums and exhibitions. Here are some notable ones to explore:

1. **Musée Ernest Cognacq:**

   - Located in Saint-Martin-de-Ré, this museum is named after the island's famous native, Ernest Cognacq. It offers a comprehensive look at the history and heritage of Île de Ré, including its maritime traditions, archaeology, and art collections.

2. **Citadelle de Saint-Martin-de-Ré**:

   - While not a traditional museum, this historic fortification in Saint-Martin-de-Ré is a UNESCO World Heritage Site and serves as a living museum. Explore the citadel's architecture and history, including its role as a former military prison.

3. **L'Abbaye des Châteliers**:

   - This abbey, located near La Flotte, is an archaeological site that offers insights into the island's medieval history. Explore the remains of the abbey, including its chapel and cloisters, and learn about its historical significance.

4. **Le Porte des Campani**:

- Located in Ars-en-Ré, this historical site features an exhibition center that delves into the history and traditions of the village and its salt production. It's a great place to learn about the island's unique heritage.

5. **Ars-en-Ré Salt Marshes Museum (Musée du Sel):**

- Discover the history of salt production on Île de Ré at this museum in Ars-en-Ré. Learn about the traditional methods of harvesting salt from the island's salt marshes and the importance of this industry.

6. **Maritime Museum of Île de Ré (Musée Maritime de l'Île de Ré):**

- Located in the village of Saint-Clement-des-Baleines, this museum explores the island's maritime history, including its fishing traditions and seafaring heritage.

7. **Chai au Quai**:

- Located in Saint-Martin-de-Ré, this wine museum offers a glimpse into the island's wine-making history. Explore the wine cellars and learn about the island's vineyards and wine production.

8. **Temporary Exhibitions:**

- Île de Ré often hosts temporary exhibitions that cover various aspects of its history and culture. Check with local tourist offices and cultural centers for information on current exhibitions.

These historical museums and exhibitions provide a deeper understanding of Île de Ré's rich heritage, from its maritime history to its cultural traditions. They are an excellent way to immerse yourself in the island's past while enjoying its natural beauty.

– Seasonal festivals and events

Île de Ré comes alive with seasonal festivals and events throughout the year. Here are some of the most anticipated celebrations on the island:

1. **Fête de la Mer (Sea Festival):**

   - Held in various villages, this festival celebrates the island's strong connection to the sea. You can enjoy seafood tastings, boat parades, fishing competitions, and live music. It's a vibrant event that showcases the island's maritime culture.

2. **Fête du Coquillage (Shellfish Festival):**

   - This seafood festival in Ars-en-Ré is a seafood lover's paradise. It features stalls selling fresh oysters, mussels, and other shellfish, as well as live music and entertainment. It's a delicious way to experience local flavors.

3. **La Flotte en Ré Festival:**

   - La Flotte hosts a variety of events throughout the year, including art exhibitions, music performances, and cultural celebrations. Check the local calendar for details on upcoming festivals and activities in La Flotte.

4. **Les Nuits Musicales en Ré (Musical Nights in Ré):**

   - This music festival, held during the summer months, features classical and contemporary music performances in historic venues across the island. It's a wonderful opportunity to enjoy music in a unique setting.

5. Les Rencontres Musicales de l'Abbaye des Châteliers (Musical Encounters at the Abbey):

- Enjoy classical and chamber music concerts in the tranquil surroundings of the Abbaye des Châteliers. These musical encounters offer a serene and cultural experience.

6. Les Journées du Patrimoine (Heritage Days):

- During France's Heritage Days, Île de Ré opens its doors to historical sites and landmarks that are not usually accessible to the public. It's a chance to explore hidden gems and learn more about the island's history.

7. Christmas Markets and Festivities:

- The holiday season on Île de Ré is a magical time. Experience Christmas markets, light displays, and festive activities in various villages. It's a charming way to celebrate the season.

8. Bike Festivals:

- Île de Ré is a cycling paradise, and several bike festivals take place during the year. These events include bike races, guided tours, and activities for cyclists of all levels.

9. Les Internationales de la Photographie en Île de Ré (International Photography Festival):

- This photography festival features exhibitions by renowned photographers and emerging talents. It's a must-visit for photography enthusiasts.

10. **Beach Parties and Fireworks:**

- During the summer months, many villages on the island host beach parties with live music, dance, and spectacular fireworks displays. It's a fantastic way to enjoy warm summer nights.

Please note that event dates and details may vary from year to year, so it's a good idea to check with local tourist offices or event organizers for the most up-to-date information on seasonal festivals and events on Île de Ré.

– Local Norms

Understanding the local norms and customs can greatly enhance your experience on Île de Ré Island. Here are some key aspects to keep in mind:

Greetings and Communication:

1. Greetings: In France, it's customary to greet people with a handshake or a kiss on the cheek (known as "la bise"). The number of kisses varies by region, but on Île de Ré, it's typically two kisses.

2. Language: While French is the official language, many locals also speak English, especially in tourist areas. However, making an effort to speak a few words of French is always appreciated.

3. Politeness: Politeness is highly valued in French culture. Saying "please" ("s'il vous plaît") and "thank you" ("merci") is important in interactions with locals.

Social Norms:

1. Personal Space: French people generally value their personal space. Avoid standing too close to others and respect their privacy.

2. Punctuality: Being on time is important in France. Whether it's for a meeting, a dinner reservation, or a social gathering, try to arrive punctually.

3. Respect for Property: Respect for public and private property is crucial. Avoid littering, keep noise levels down, and follow local regulations.

4. Queueing: In public places like markets or shops, it's customary to wait in line (queue) for service. Cutting in line is considered rude.

5. Dress Code: While the dress code on Île de Ré is generally casual, it's respectful to dress neatly when visiting churches, upscale restaurants, or attending special events.

Dining and Food:

1. Meal Times: Lunch is typically served between 12:00 p.m. and 2:00 p.m., and dinner between 7:00 p.m. and 9:00 p.m. on Île de Ré, although times can vary.

2. Table Manners: Follow the French dining etiquette, such as keeping your hands visible above the table, using utensils appropriately, and not starting to eat until everyone is served.

3. Tipping: While a service charge is often included in the bill, it's customary to leave a small additional tip for good service (around 5-10%).

Environmental and Cultural Awareness:

1. Environmental Conservation: The island's natural beauty is cherished by locals. Help preserve it by avoiding littering, respecting wildlife, and following designated paths in natural areas.

2. Cultural Sites: Show respect when visiting cultural and historic sites. Follow the rules and regulations, and be mindful of the significance of these places to the local community.

Socializing and Events:

1. Local Events: Embrace the local culture by participating in festivals, markets, and other events. It's a great way to immerse yourself in the community and learn about the island's traditions.

2. Socializing: French people enjoy socializing over meals and drinks. Invitations to homes are common and are a great way to experience local hospitality.

By adhering to these local norms, you can show respect for the island's culture and community and have a more enriching experience during your visit to Île de Ré Island, France.

Chapter 8: Accommodations

– Range from luxury hotels to bed and breakfasts

Île de Ré offers a diverse range of accommodations to suit different preferences and budgets, from luxurious hotels to charming bed and breakfasts.

Luxury Hotels

1. Le Clos Saint-Martin Hotel & Spa: This luxury hotel offers a serene environment with well-appointed rooms and a spa. It's an ideal spot for relaxation and pampering. Prices generally start around €250 per night.

2. Hôtel de Toiras: Located by the picturesque harbor of Saint-Martin-de-Ré, this hotel combines historical elegance with modern amenities. Expect to pay starting from €180 per night.

3. Villa Clarisse: Nestled in Saint-Martin-de-Ré, this hotel offers privacy and luxury, with easy access to the island's attractions. Nightly rates begin at approximately €200.

Mid-Range and Boutique Hotels

1. Hôtel Le Sénéchal: Situated in Ars-en-Ré, this hotel provides a unique atmosphere with its individually decorated rooms and proximity to local markets. Room prices start at about €150 per night.

2. La Baronnie Hôtel & Spa: A historical setting surrounded by gardens, offering a spa and personal service, with rooms from €170 per night.

Bed and Breakfasts

1. Le Soleil Do' Ré: This B&B in Sainte-Marie-de-Ré is well-liked for its comfort and location, with nightly rates typically around €100.

2. LE LANTERNON: Located in Saint-Martin-de-Ré, this B&B offers fabulous hospitality and has a rustic charm, with prices starting near €95 per night.

3. Les Chênes Bleus: Another excellent choice in Sainte-Marie-de-Ré, known for its tranquil setting and quality service, with rates beginning at about €90 per night.

Budget Options

1. Camping La Grainetière: For a less traditional stay, this campsite offers mobile homes and quirky wooden wagons, providing a budget-friendly option with a unique twist. Prices for mobile homes start at approximately €50 per night.

2. Vacation Rentals: Various properties on Airbnb provide a more personal accommodation experience, with options ranging from cozy apartments to spacious homes. Prices vary, but a typical apartment might cost around €100 per night depending on the season and exact location.

This range of options ensures that whether you're looking for luxury, a cozy B&B vibe, or a budget-friendly stay, Île de Ré has something to offer every traveler. Always check the latest prices and availability directly with the accommodations or through reputable booking platforms.

– Recommendations for different budgets and preferences

Île de Ré, a picturesque island off the west coast of France, is a popular destination known for its serene beaches, salt marshes, and quaint villages. Catering to diverse tastes and budgets, here are some tailored recommendations for accommodation and activities:

Luxury: Indulge in Elegance

Accommodation: Opt for Le Clos Saint-Martin Hotel & Spa or Hôtel de Toiras which offers luxury stays with spa facilities and gourmet dining. These hotels provide the ultimate relaxation experience with rooms typically starting from €180 to €250 per night.

Activities: Rent a yacht for a day of sailing, or enjoy guided tours of local vineyards. High-end dining options abound, particularly seafood and local delicacies like the salt marsh lamb.

Mid-Range: Comfort and Culture

Accommodation: Hôtel Le Sénéchal in Ars-en-Ré and La Baronnie Hôtel & Spa offer a great mix of comfort and local charm with rates starting around €150 to €170 per night.

Activities: Explore the island's cycle paths with rented bikes, visit historical sites like the Fortifications of Vauban, and taste local oysters directly from the oyster farms.

Budget-Friendly: Affordable Explorations

Accommodation: Camping La Grainetière provides an affordable option with mobile homes and pitches for tents, with rates as low as €50 per night. Budget hotels and hostels are also available, offering basic amenities and a friendly atmosphere.

Activities: Hiking and beachcombing are cost-free and allow you to appreciate the island's natural beauty. Visit local markets for affordable fresh produce and seafood.

Bed and Breakfasts: Homely Feel

Accommodation: Stay at a B&B like Le Soleil Do' Ré or Les Chênes Bleus for a more intimate experience, with rates generally around €90 to €100 per night.

Activities: Engage with your hosts to learn about the local way of life. Many B&Bs offer bike rentals, which is a perfect way to explore the island's quaint villages and harbors.

For Families: Kid-Friendly Choices

Accommodation: Family-friendly hotels like Hotel Le Peu Breton offer amenities such as pools and play areas, ensuring a stay that is comfortable for both adults and children.

Activities: Visit the donkey farm, where children can interact with the famously trousered donkeys of the island, or spend a day at the beach flying kites and building sandcastles.

For Couples: Romantic Getaways

Accommodation: Choose a secluded cottage or a charming suite in a boutique hotel to enjoy privacy with a romantic setting.

Activities: Take sunset walks along the beaches, dine at intimate restaurants, and enjoy a couple's massages at local spas.

These options cater to a range of preferences and budgets, ensuring that every visitor can find the perfect way to experience the charm of Île de Ré. Whether seeking relaxation, adventure, or cultural immersion, this beautiful island offers a comprehensive array of activities and accommodations. Always check for the most current prices and availability to plan

Chapter 9: Practical Information

– Language and currency

Currency

Île de Ré, located off the west coast of France, utilizes the Euro (€) as its official currency, in line with the rest of France. Here is a comprehensive guide on currency and money management for those planning to visit Île de Ré:

Currency Basics

- Currency Used: The Euro (€, EUR) is the only currency accepted in Île de Ré. It is divided into 100 cents.

- Denominations: Euro banknotes come in 5, 10, 20, 50, 100, 200, and 500 denominations, although the 200 and 500 euro notes are less commonly used and accepted. Coins come in 1, 2, 5, 10, 20, and 50 cents, as well as 1 and 2 euro denominations.

Exchanging Money

- Before Arrival: It's often wise to exchange some money into Euros before leaving for Île de Ré to avoid potentially higher exchange rates and fees at airports or local exchange offices.

You can do this at most major banks or through a currency exchange service in your home country.

- On the Island: Additional exchanges can be made at banks on the island, which usually offer better rates than exchange offices. Ensure you check operating hours as these can be limited, especially outside of peak tourist seasons.

Using Credit Cards and ATMs

- Credit Cards: Major credit cards (Visa, MasterCard, American Express) are widely accepted in hotels, most restaurants, and shops. It's a good idea to inform your card issuer about your travel plans to prevent your card from being flagged for suspicious activity.

- ATMs: These are readily available in Île de Ré, particularly in larger towns. They offer a convenient way to withdraw cash as needed, generally providing better exchange rates compared to currency exchange points. Be aware of possible transaction fees, which vary depending on your bank's policies.

Money Management Tips

- Budgeting: Plan your budget considering average prices on the island. Dining out, accommodation, and activities can vary greatly in price, so it helps to research and plan accordingly.

- Cash vs. Card: While card payments are common, having cash is essential for smaller cafes, markets, or in case of card machine failures. It's particularly important when visiting remote areas or for using local transportation.

- Safety: As with any travel destination, keep your money and cards secure. Use hotel safes when available, and carry only what you need for the day.

- Financial Institutions: If staying for an extended period, be aware that the local banks can provide currency exchange, banking services, and financial advice suitable for tourists.

Emergency Contacts

- Lost or Stolen Cards: Always have a list of emergency numbers for your bank to quickly block any lost or stolen cards. Additionally, keeping a digital copy of important documents in a secure place online can save a lot of trouble.

By preparing appropriately with the right mix of cash and card accessibility, you can ensure a smooth financial experience on Île de Ré. This enables you to enjoy the stunning landscapes, cultural experiences, and gastronomic delights without worrying about money matters.

Language

Île de Ré, like the rest of France, primarily uses French as its official language. For travelers, understanding some basic

French phrases and words can greatly enhance the experience, making interactions with locals smoother and more engaging. Here's a comprehensive guide to the language and communication essentials for Île de Ré:

Basic French Phrases and Words

- Hello: "Bonjour" (bon-ZHOOR)

- Goodbye: "Au revoir" (oh ruh-VWAHR)

- Please: "S'il vous plaît" (seel voo PLEH)

- Thank you: "Merci" (mehr-SEE)

- Yes: "Oui" (wee)

- No: "Non" (nohn)

- Excuse me/Sorry: "Pardon" or "Excusez-moi" (ex-kew-ZAY mwah)

- Do you speak English?: "Parlez-vous anglais?" (par-LAY voo ahn-GLAY?)

- I don't understand: "Je ne comprends pas" (zhuh nuh kom-PRAHN pah)

- How much is this?: "Combien ça coûte?" (kohm-BYEN sah koot?)

- Where is...?: "Où est...?" (ooh eh...?)

- Bathroom: "Toilettes" (twah-LET)

- Help!: "Au secours!" (oh suh-KOOR!)

Pronunciation Tips

French pronunciation can be tricky due to its nasal sounds and silent letters. Here are a few tips:

- Nasal vowels: These are common in French and are pronounced by allowing air to escape through the nose, as in "non" (nohn).

- Silent letters: Many French words end with consonants that are not pronounced unless followed by a word that begins with a vowel, which is called liaison.

- Accents: French uses several accents that can change the pronunciation of letters, especially vowels. For example, 'é' (acute accent) as in 'café' (kah-FAY) is more open than 'e'.

Communication Essentials

- Gestures: French people often use expressive gestures during conversation. A simple smile or nod can go a long way in non-verbal communication.

- Formality: French language and culture place a high value on formality and politeness. Always use "s'il vous plaît" (please) and "merci" (thank you) to show courtesy.

- Local dialects: While standard French is widely understood, some local expressions or regional variations might be present. Listening to locals can provide insights into regional nuances.

Language Learning Resources

To further enhance your language skills before or during your trip, consider the following:

- Language apps: Apps like Duolingo, Babbel, or Rosetta Stone can provide basic French language training.

- Phrasebooks: Carry a French phrasebook or download a language app specifically for travel-related phrases.

- Local interaction: Practice speaking French with locals, as real-world usage is one of the best ways to learn.

Understanding and using these basic phrases and pronunciation tips will not only help you navigate Île de Ré more easily but also enrich your interaction with the local culture and people. The effort to speak even a little French is often appreciated and can make your experience more enjoyable and authentic.

– Travel tips and essential information

Here are some travel tips and essential information to make your visit to Île de Ré a smooth and enjoyable experience:

1. **Best Time to Visit**:

   - The peak tourist season on the island is during the summer months (June to August). If you prefer fewer crowds and milder weather, consider visiting in the shoulder seasons of spring (April to May) and fall (September to October).

2. Cycling is Key:

- Île de Ré is known for its excellent cycling infrastructure. Rent a bicycle to explore the island's villages, beaches, and natural beauty. There are numerous bike rental shops, and many accommodations offer bike rentals as well.

3. Toll Bridge (Pont de l'île de Ré):

- Note that there is a toll bridge to access the island. Be prepared to pay the toll, and consider the traffic during peak travel times.

4. Reservations:

- During the high season, it's advisable to make reservations for accommodations, restaurants, and activities well in advance, especially if you have specific preferences.

5. Beaches and Sunscreen:

- Île de Ré boasts beautiful beaches, so don't forget your sunscreen, beach towels, and swimwear.

6. Local Cuisine:

- Be sure to savor the local seafood, oysters, and salt marsh lamb during your visit. Explore the island's markets for fresh produce and artisanal products.

7. Cash and Cards:

- While credit and debit cards are widely accepted, it's a good idea to carry some cash for small purchases and places that may not accept cards.

8. **Language**:

- French is the primary language spoken on the island. Learning a few basic French phrases can be helpful when interacting with locals.

9. **Transportation**:

- Île de Ré is easily accessible by car, but consider using bicycles or public transportation to explore the island, as parking can be limited in some areas.

10. Pet-Friendly Island:

- Île de Ré is known for being pet-friendly, so you can often bring your furry friends along. Just check with your accommodation for their pet policy.

11. **Emergency Information**:

- Know the local emergency numbers: 112 for general emergencies, 15 for medical emergencies, and 17 for police assistance.

12. **Respect Local Customs**:

- Respect the island's natural environment and local customs. Follow designated paths and beach rules, and be mindful of wildlife and protected areas.

13. **Waste Disposal**:

- Dispose of your waste properly and recycle where available. Keep the island clean and environmentally friendly.

14. **Travel Insurance**:

- Consider purchasing travel insurance to cover unexpected events during your trip.

15. **Local Events**:

- Check the local event calendar for festivals, markets, and cultural events happening during your visit.

Île de Ré is a charming and picturesque destination with much to offer. By following these travel tips and being prepared, you can fully enjoy your time on the island and create wonderful memories.

- Emergency contacts and healthcare facilities

When visiting Île de Ré, it's important to be aware of emergency contacts and healthcare facilities in case you need assistance during your stay. Here are the essential emergency contacts and healthcare information:

Emergency Numbers:

- General Emergencies: Dial 112

- This number is used for all types of emergencies, including police, medical, and fire emergencies. It is the universal emergency number in Europe.

- **Medical Emergencies**: Dial 15

If you require immediate medical assistance, dial 15 to reach emergency medical services (SAMU). They can dispatch ambulances and provide medical advice over the phone.

- **Police and Law Enforcement**: Dial 17

- In case of a police or law enforcement emergency, dial 17 to reach the local police.

Healthcare Facilities:

- **Hôpital de La Rochelle (La Rochelle Hospital):**

  - **Address**: 2 Rue de Saint-Eloi, 17000 La Rochelle, France

  - **Phone**: +33 5 46 45 50 50

- **Pharmacies (Pharmacies in Île de Ré):**

Île de Ré has several pharmacies located in various villages. Pharmacies are generally well-equipped and can provide over-the-counter medications and medical advice.

- **Medical Practices and Clinics**:

There are medical practices and clinics on the island where you can consult with doctors for non-emergency medical issues.

- **Dentists**:

If you require dental care, there are dental clinics and practitioners available on Île de Ré.

It's advisable to have travel insurance that covers medical emergencies when visiting Île de Ré. Additionally, keep a list of your important medical information, including allergies and any required medications, in case you need medical attention during your stay.

While Île de Ré is generally a safe destination, being aware of emergency contacts and healthcare facilities ensures that you are prepared for any unforeseen situations during your visit.

– Do's and Don'ts

Île de Ré Island, France: Do's and Don'ts

Do's:

1. Explore the Beaches: Enjoy the island's beautiful beaches, such as Plage de la Conche des Baleines and Plage des Gollandières, for sunbathing and swimming.

2. Cycling: Rent a bicycle and explore the island's picturesque villages, salt marshes, and vineyards along the extensive network of cycle paths.

3. Visit the Villages: Discover the charming villages of Saint-Martin-de-Ré, Ars-en-Ré, and La Flotte, known for their historic architecture, markets, and seafood restaurants.

4. Try Local Cuisine: Sample fresh seafood, including oysters, mussels, and fish, as well as the island's renowned potatoes and salt.

5. Visit Fortifications: Explore the island's historic fortifications, including Fort Boyard and the Vauban fortifications in Saint-Martin-de-Ré, a UNESCO World Heritage site.

6. Shop at Markets: Visit local markets for fresh produce, artisanal products, and souvenirs, such as the market in La Flotte or the daily market in Sainte-Marie-de-Ré.

7. Attend Events: Experience local festivals and events, such as the Sea Salt Festival in Ars-en-Ré or the La Flotte en Ré Jazz Festival.

8. Enjoy Nature: Explore the island's natural beauty at the Lilleau des Niges Nature Reserve or the Phare des Baleines lighthouse.

9. Respect the Environment: Follow designated paths, avoid disturbing wildlife, and dispose of waste properly to protect the island's natural environment.

10. Learn the History: Visit museums and historic sites to learn about the island's rich history, including its maritime heritage and role in the salt trade.

Don'ts:

1. Overcrowd Beaches: Avoid overcrowding beaches, especially during peak tourist seasons, to respect other visitors and the environment.

2. Ignore Traffic Rules: Follow traffic rules, especially when cycling, to ensure your safety and the safety of others on the island.

3. Litter: Dispose of waste properly and recycle whenever possible to maintain the island's cleanliness and beauty.

4. Damage Wildlife: Avoid disturbing wildlife, such as nesting birds or seals, and observe them from a safe distance.

5. Disrespect Locals: Be respectful to locals and their customs, including greetings and manners, to foster positive interactions.

6. Ignore Cycling Etiquette: Follow cycling etiquette, such as signaling and yielding to pedestrians, to ensure a safe and pleasant experience for everyone.

7. Disregard Natural Areas: Stay on designated paths in natural areas to avoid damaging fragile ecosystems.

8. Forget Sun Protection: Use sunscreen and protective clothing to prevent sunburn and skin damage, especially during the sunny summer months.

9. Miss Local Events: Take advantage of opportunities to experience local culture, such as festivals and markets, to immerse yourself in the island's unique atmosphere.

10. Be Unaware of Tides: Be aware of tidal schedules when visiting beaches to avoid being stranded or caught by rising tides.

By following these do's and don'ts, you can have a memorable and enjoyable visit to Île de Ré Island, France, while respecting its environment, culture, and local communities.

Chapter 10: FAQs

- Common questions about travel logistics, activities, and local customs

Here are answers to some common questions about travel logistics, activities, and local customs on Île de Ré:

1. Is it necessary to book accommodations in advance?

- During the peak tourist season (summer months), it's advisable to book accommodations in advance, especially if you have specific preferences. However, during the shoulder seasons, you may find more availability without advanced reservations.

2. Can I rent bicycles on the island, and are there bike trails?

- Yes, you can rent bicycles on Île de Ré, and the island is known for its excellent cycling infrastructure. There are dedicated bike trails that connect villages, beaches, and natural attractions.

3. What are the best beaches on the island?

- Île de Ré offers numerous beautiful beaches. Some popular ones include Le Bois-Plage-en-Ré, La Plage de la Cible, and

Les Grenettes. Each beach has its unique charm, so explore and find your favorite.

4. Are dogs allowed on the beaches?

- Île de Ré is known for being pet-friendly, and many beaches allow dogs. However, there may be specific rules and leash requirements in certain areas, so it's best to check with local authorities.

5. What is the toll for the bridge to Île de Ré (Pont de l'île de Ré)?

- The toll for the bridge varies depending on the type of vehicle and the season. It's a good idea to check the current toll rates before your trip.

6. Are there restrictions on where to park on the island?

- Yes, parking can be limited in some areas, especially during the peak season. Look for designated parking areas and follow parking regulations to avoid fines.

7. What are the local customs and etiquette on the island?

- Be respectful of the natural environment and wildlife. Stay on designated paths, follow beach rules, and dispose of waste properly. When interacting with locals, polite greetings and basic French phrases are appreciated.

8. Can I swim in the sea all year round?

- While swimming is possible during the summer months when the water is warmer, some visitors also enjoy swimming in the shoulder seasons. Be mindful of water safety and local conditions.

9. Are there supermarkets and grocery stores on the island?

- Yes, you'll find supermarkets and grocery stores in various villages on Île de Ré, making it convenient to purchase supplies and groceries for your stay.

10. What's the best way to explore the island's villages?

- Bicycles are a popular and eco-friendly way to explore the island's villages. You can also use public transportation or rent a car if preferred.

11. Are there any restrictions on photography or drone usage?

- While photography is generally allowed, be respectful of private property and people's privacy. As for drones, there may be restrictions in certain areas, so check local regulations before flying.

12. What are the opening hours for shops and restaurants?

- Shop and restaurant opening hours may vary, but typically, shops are open in the morning and early evening, with a break during the afternoon. Restaurants often open for lunch and dinner service. It's a good idea to check specific hours with individual establishments.

These answers to common questions should help you plan your trip to Île de Ré with confidence and ensure a smooth and enjoyable experience. Safe Trip!

Map

Printed in Great Britain
by Amazon

41634029R00059